Exploring Earth and Space

by Wolf Shelton

PEARSON
Scott
Foresman

DK

The Sun

Stars are made of hot, glowing gases. The Sun is a star. It is made of hot, glowing gases.

The Sun is the closest star to Earth. This is why it looks bigger and brighter than other stars. The Sun is so big and bright that you cannot see other stars during the day.

a flare of hot gas
from the Sun

This is a photo of the Sun in space.

We Need the Sun

The Sun is much larger than Earth. It looks small in the sky because it is very far away. One million Earths could fit inside the Sun!

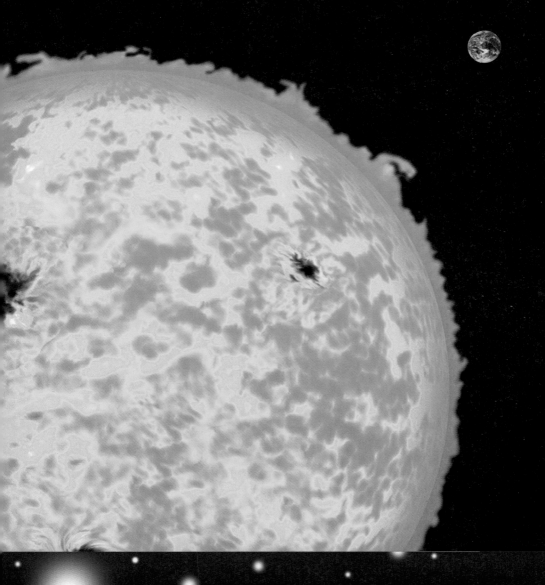

The Sun is important for life on Earth.
The Sun gives heat and light. People, plants,
and animals need heat and light to live.

Day and Night

This picture shows a line through the center of Earth. The line is not real. It is imaginary. It is called Earth's **axis.**

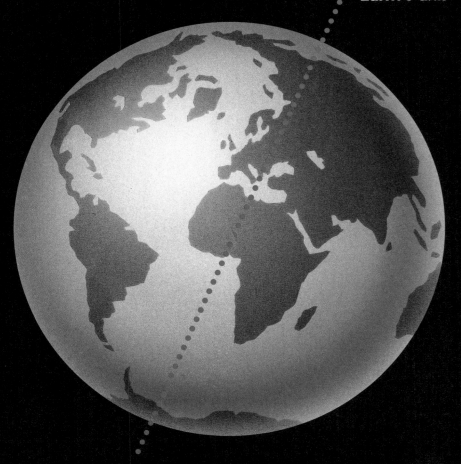

Earth's axis

6

Earth is always moving in a circle around its axis. Moving around an axis is called **rotation.** Each day Earth makes one rotation.

Earth rotates, or moves, around its axis.

Day and night happen because Earth rotates.

For some hours, the part of Earth where you live faces the Sun. Then it is daytime for you. For some hours, the part of Earth where you live faces away from the Sun. Then it is nighttime for you.

light from the Sun

Can you see where it is daytime? Can you see where it is nighttime?

Why does the Sun move in the sky?

The Sun looks like it moves in the sky. It does not really move. Earth turns on its axis and moves in and out of the Sun's light. This makes it seem like the Sun is moving across the sky.

In the morning when the Sun rises, it is low in the sky. We talk about the Sun coming up, but really, the part of Earth where you live is just moving into the Sun's light.

At noon the Sun looks like it is in the middle of the sky.

sunrise

In the evening, it may look like the Sun is moving down. Really, the part of Earth where you live is moving out of the Sun's light. The Sun does not go away. It shines on the other side of Earth. You just cannot see it where you live.

noon Sun

sunset

Seasons

Earth is tilted on its axis. Earth also moves around the Sun. It takes one year for Earth to move all the way around the Sun. Earth's path around the Sun is called its orbit. Earth's tilt and its orbit around the Sun make seasons happen.

Here it is summer for people living in the top half of Earth.

When the part of Earth where you live tilts toward the Sun, it is summer or spring. When the part of Earth where you live tilts away from the Sun, you have winter or fall.

Here it is winter for people living in the top half of Earth.

The Night Sky

You can see the constellation Orion in the sky. Find the three bright stars in a line that make his belt.

The Sun is a huge star close to Earth. This is why you can see the Sun in the daytime. You can see other stars at night. They look smaller than the Sun because they are very far away.

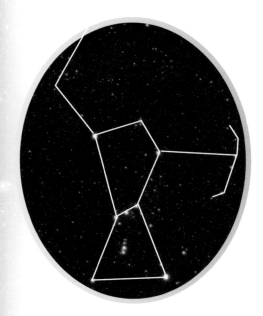

The bright stars in Orion make the shape of a hunter.

People made up stories about stars. They imagined lines connecting groups of stars, like a game of "Connect the Dots." Each picture they saw is called a **constellation.** Constellations are groups of stars.

The Moon

The Moon is the brightest object we can see in the night sky. Sometimes you can see the Moon in the daytime.

the Moon in the daytime

The Moon has deep craters. A **crater** is a big hole. Large rocks from space crashed into the Moon and made craters. The Moon also has mountains.

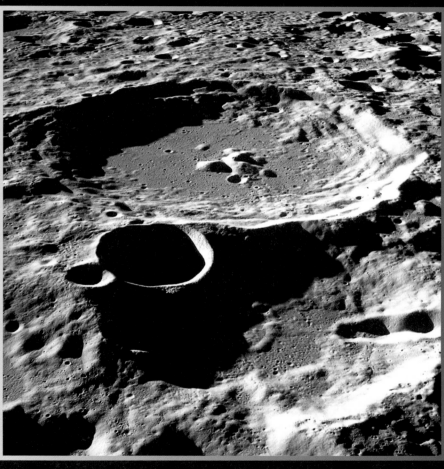

The Moon's Changes

Earth moves in an orbit around the Sun. At the same time, the Moon moves in an orbit around Earth. It takes about four weeks for the Moon to make one orbit around Earth.

Can you trace Earth's orbit and the Moon's orbit with your finger?

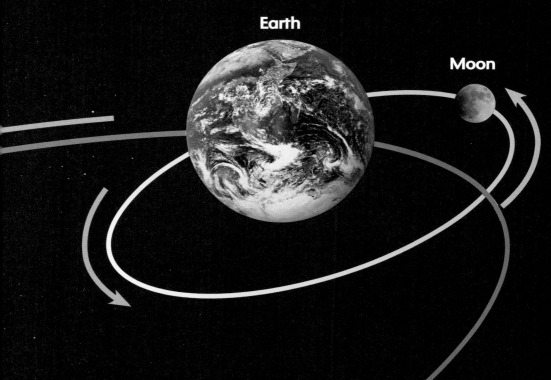

Earth

Moon

The Moon looks like it changes shape each night. Really, the Moon always stays the same shape. When you see the Moon from Earth you are seeing light from the Sun falling on the Moon in different ways.

Sometimes the Moon looks like a circle. You are looking at the lit side of the Moon.
   Sometimes the Sun only shines on a part of the Moon.

Sometimes you cannot see the Moon at all. This is because you are looking at the side of the Moon that is not lit.

The shape of the part of the Moon that you see is called a phase.

The Solar System

The solar system is everything that moves, or orbits, around the Sun. This includes the eight planets and their moons. Earth is one of the eight planets.

Saturn

Mars

Venus

Sun

Mercury

Earth

Look at the picture of our solar system. Can you find the Sun in the middle? Can you name the other planets?

Jupiter

Uranus

Neptune

Glossary

axis an imaginary line through the center of Earth

constellation a group of stars that form a picture

crater a bowl-shaped hole on a moon or planet made by crashing rocks

orbit a path around something

phase the Moon's shape that we can see

rotation movement around an axis

solar system the nine planets and other objects that orbit around the Sun